# A
# View
# From The
# Piano Bench

Topos Books is an imprint of Topos Productions

TOPOS PRODUCTIONS
1050 Queen Street, Suite 100
Honolulu, HI 96814
USA

toposproductions.com

ISBN-13: 978-1-943354-01-6
ISBN-10: 1-943354-01-4

Kelly Park

# A
# View
# From The
# Piano Bench

## A Case for Intellectual Music

With a Foreword by Mads Tolling
Edited by Holger R. Heine

# Contents

## Chapter 5

## Appendix

## About the Author

# Foreword

Mads Tolling

I first met Kelly Park in San Francisco six years ago while playing a gig with singer and songwriter Danny Givertz. The set list was full of pop, rock, and folk type tunes. Kelly handled the percussion and drum set like a pro, and we struck up a nice friendship. We had the love for Denmark in common. I grew up there and Kelly lived there a few years back in the day. Kelly knew a few Danish phrases – most which had to do with food. We also had in common that we both are jazz musicians. So why of all things were we playing on a singer songwriter gig in San Francisco?

One of the special aspects of playing jazz is the training and the background you need to have to play it. You can't just walk in from the street to play jazz – there is no American Idol contest for playing jazz, and for good reason. Jazz is not for overnight sensations – it is more of a marathon than a sprint. And you have to apply yourself early on and keep learning – basically until you die.

I grew up in Copenhagen, Denmark, and started playing the violin at age six. I was going to be a classical musician, until the beautiful sounds of Miles Davis grabbed me at age 14. That experience transformed me and made me want to learn how it was done. I eventually was able to go to a special music high school that both offered courses in classical and jazz and later I moved to Boston to study jazz at Berklee College of Music. Berklee is a school where you can study anything from DJ'ing to musical therapy to the music of Stevie Wonder. In other words, Berklee is a very well-rounded program that in many ways is perfect for a life in music. Why? Because it offers a taste into a lot of different aspects of music. Kelly Park is a Berklee graduate too. Berklee's mission and the students it sets out in the world of music offer a big part of the explanation why Kelly and I, two jazz musicians, were able to "hang" doing a singer songwriter gig that evening in San Francisco.

What jazz offers is something truly unique that no other genre of music offers. This is why jazz musicians like bassist Christian McBride can play with Sting and why the Count Basie Orchestra was the perfect match for Frank Sinatra. To play jazz you have to have a very high level of craft on your instrument – you have to have put in the 10,000 hours of practice to sound good and to have the dexterity and freedom on your instrument. Jazz offers a deep understanding of harmony, but it doesn't skip the very basic harmony like I – IV – V progressions. Many jazz tunes are written with very simple harmonic progressions, such as Blue Monk by Thelonious Monk or C Jam Blues by Duke Ellington. Each just with three chords, not much more than a nursery rhyme. But then jazz can also go to the extreme like John Coltrane's Giants Steps and Countdown. So, to play jazz you need to master the simple as well as the complex.

Jazz is in essence a mix of European functional harmony and African Rhythms, and what really sets jazz apart from European classical music is the rhythm. Jazz has a groove to it, and this groove can be quite complex, in time signatures of 5/4, 7/4, 13/8, 20/4, you name it. In European classical music the rhythm is generally very basic and "ungroovy," and most classical musicians, although theoretically able to play complex rhythms, have a very undeveloped sense of groove and rhythmic feel.

Needless to say you won't be playing a lot of 13/8 on a pop gig, but your ability to groove and swing, which jazz gives you, is a huge help that people in the classical world lack. When learning how to play classical music you are told not to tap your foot. In jazz you have to tap your foot, when you learn, or you will never get the right feel.

Jazz musicians also have the ability to improvise, which comes from both the knowledge of rhythm and harmony. All these abilities really make jazz musicians the go-to-person for a lot of recording work, freelance, and teaching gigs. Since being able to master jazz, you essentially have to be able to master all the elements that goes into 95 percent of the music heard on the radio today. Most jazz musicians can go out and play on a pop, rock, country, hip hop, latin or funk gig anytime. And the learning curve is significantly shorter for say a jazz musician learning to play hip hop vs. a hip hop artist learning to play jazz, since all the elements found in hip hop music more or less can also be found in jazz, but not the other way around.

To me this makes jazz the music form that should be taught to children of all ages, and adding to it that jazz is a uniquely American invention, it should have more gravitas than it currently has.

I came to the US to study jazz where it was born. I initially thought that the Abercrombie and Fitch T-shirts were for guitar player John Abercrombie, who is hardly, I later realized, a household name in the US. I learned from my experiences in this country that being well rounded and being a "jack of all trades" can be a great way to go and be very fulfilling. If I hadn't I am not sure I would have met Kelly Park on that singer songwriter gig on a summer evening in San Francisco.

# Chapter 1

## Observations On The Nature Of Things

### Introduction

"The best in music is not found in the notes" – Gustav Mahler

This little book is a collection of things that have rattled around in my mind for a long time. It has been cathartic to actually write them down and take the time to flesh them out. In some cases I'd write something down and realize that I didn't really think that way at all, I just hadn't thought it through enough to see the logic flaws, or bad attitudes, or just the plain stupidity of the thought, attitude, or idea onto which I'd been holding for so long. So if you come across any logic flaws, bad attitudes, or just plain stupidity in reading this, please forgive me.

Welcome to my brain.

# Conversations #1

"Without music, life would be a mistake" – Friedrich Wilhelm Nietzsche

I carry on imaginary conversations, interviews, arguments and so on with existing or fictitious persons. This all happens in my head. Usually while driving, showering, or playing the piano. These conversations usually reflect my view(s) on some topic that has arisen at a point in time close to when the (imaginary) conversation takes place, but some of these go back to earliest childhood.

For instance:

The Scene: A TV studio with a table set-up at which I and the show's host are seated (somewhat like the show "Inside the Actor's Studio" on Bravo), with an enraptured audience hanging on every word.

Interviewer ("I" from now on) (into the camera): "Good evening, ladies and gentlemen. Tonight, we're visiting with pianist Kelly Park, exploring the world of music from his point of view. Most of you are aware that he is a jazz pianist, so the focus of tonight's discussion will be on jazz and maybe going a little further afield into the broader world of popular music. His professional credits speak for themselves; he holds a Bachelor's of Music in Jazz Composition and Arranging from the Berklee College of Music and was a faculty member of Berklee as well, teaching jazz, harmony, theory, and arranging. He has traveled the world over playing music and has been a professional musician, making his living by playing and writing music, for some thirty-five years."

(Turns to me.)

"So, Kelly, let's begin tonight's discussion with a statement from you about how you go about creating music, either from a compositional standpoint, an improvisational standpoint, or any other, well . . . er . . . *standpoint* you'd care to discuss."

(A small titter from the audience.)

Me, after a moment's thought: "Well, Stan (his name is Stan for no particular reason) let me say that first, and foremost, I believe jazz is a creation of the moment. An expression of the player's feeling towards the sounds that surround him at that particular moment in time. This is why a player may sound one way on a tune one night, and the next night play it completely differently.

The framework upon which this "creation of the moment" is hung may be a static, prearranged number of bars and order of chord changes, but the player with open ears, mind, and heart finds something new in it every time he plays it. This is the essence of jazz, its special magic that sets it apart from many other musical forms."

I (Isn't it interesting that the two characters having this conversation are "I" and "Me?" It just worked out that way): "So you think that jazz has a special magic that other musical forms don't?"

Me: "No, I think that all music has some sort of magic about it or it wouldn't survive the test of time. It just so happens that I believe that, beyond the advanced harmony, complex rhythm, and subtleties of tone and dynamics, the creation of this 'sound of now' is at the heart of jazz music.

I have often heard jazz played by very accomplished musicians, playing very advanced music that falls a little flat on my ears because of the lack of this (what I believe to be) essential quality. I can still appreciate the technical abilities of the players and the dissonances that tickle my ears, but I need that spontaneity. I also think that most of the greatest jazz recordings capture an echo of this spark."

I: "I see. So you say that all music has some sort of magic. What is the magic of, say, heavy metal rock to you?"

Me: "Well, Stan, in my view, almost all popular music is only partially about the music. There are social and cultural aspects to many forms of music that are stronger and more vital to the success and survival of that music than there are in jazz .

The most obvious may be the rap and hip-hop of the last several years. Where would that music be without the bling? The cars? The women? I don't think it would have captured the imagination of so many millions of people had it not had the trappings of money and sex that it so prominently displays.

Or take country western. The demographic of country western fans is fairly easy to see. Eighty percent (just to put a number on it) white, lower-to-upper-middle-class people.

The people to whom jazz appeals, conversely, come from a much broader spectrum, you've got wealthy suburbanites, poor inner-city youth, introverted music nerds, extroverted, enthusiastic college kids, Europeans, Japanese, South Americans , and everybody in between. I don't think jazz can be tied to a social, racial, or economic group as tightly as most other types of music can."

I: "And again, the magic of heavy metal?"

(Another small titter.)

Me: "OK, heavy metal. Well, I think one needs only to go to the marketing and advertising people to get the demographics of just about any genre of music. What do they say for heavy metal, predominantly thirteen to thirty-year-old white males? Much of the magic of metal, I believe, would lie in its raw energy and its ability to meld itself with, and also to influence, its audience's emotional flow. Not to mention the power of sheer volume!

I think the successful metal bands have tapped into an emotional channel that strikes a chord (no pun intended) with their fans. Be that emotion rage or joy, they take their audiences on a journey. But remember, like with rap and bling, where would heavy metal be without the light show? The onstage explosions? The romanticized myth of sex, drugs, and rock and roll? I'm pretty sure that a large percentage of the people that attend metal and rock concerts are only minimally interested in the musical statements that the musicians onstage are making. I think many of them are there primarily either to just make the scene, or to be able to tell people the next day that they were there. Or to see the spectacle that is a major rock concert. Any way you look at it, the actual music, the notes being played, is only one sliver of the total experience."

I, smiling: "It almost sounds like you're a heavy metal fan."

Me, smiling back: "No, not even a little bit. Let's look at it this way. If we were to break music down into its component parts, that is, generally speaking, melody, harmony, and rhythm (and I guess we need to include lyrics, since every genre mentioned so far is pretty much a vocal music, and we should probably also include emotional message), I can show you very clearly why my attitudes about different genres of music are what they are.

I tend to rate each component part of the genre into three categories, undeveloped (by which I mean not only simple, which sometimes can be very effective in music, but actually undeveloped in the sense that to me it doesn't seem as though the person who created the music got past the basic, beginning stages in technical musical knowledge), semi-developed (obviously a step up from undeveloped), and fully developed (fully formed musical thoughts and ideas, obviously time was spent studying and honing the craft of music).

Before anybody jumps down my throat, these are not criticisms of the various genres, if I could find different words than "undeveloped" and "developed" with their attendant negative implications to use, I would. And I want to stress that this is only my way of looking at it, I'm not preaching to convert anybody, I'm not even saying that my way is the right way. It's just my own way of perceiving things.

OK, that said, if we were to take, for example, an extremely popular form of music, say, country and western, and examine it on the basis of its component parts, I'd break it down this way: melody: semi-developed, although pleasant, I don't hear most country melodies as being especially inventive or sophisticated (even in a simple way) I hear them as very "hook" oriented, in the way that nursery rhymes are very tonal and banal.

I'm sure there are many country melodies that have greater musical value than others, but for pure musicality (the melody, the notes, not the lyrics), I can't see country melodies holding up when compared to great melodists like Mozart or Bach, or American popular melodists like Gershwin or Hoagy Carmichael. Not to mention the great instrumental jazz melodists, who write melody for melody's sake, not as a vehicle for a set of words. Guys like Chick Corea, Herbie Hancock, or Dave Brubeck. I'm not just saying this as a personal preference, I'm trying to look at the different musical styles dispassionately and objectively, comparing them on musical merit alone, not my personal taste.

If the comparison seems a bit 'apples and oranges,' so be it. The notes are in the air, the music is available at the touch of a radio button, or at the click of a mouse, and I think on some level music is music, the organization of the twelve tones of Western harmony, and can stand comparison and analysis.

Harmony: undeveloped, I don't think even the country guys would argue that the harmonies used in country music are extremely basic, it's in the nature of the music. My ears like something to tickle them, some color tones that just aren't there in country music.

To use the nursery rhyme analogy again, I think there are kid's songs with more interesting harmonies than some country songs! This is not to say that some country players can't play - there have been some truly excellent instrumentalists who have chosen country (or country chose them) as their preferred medium (Glen Campbell and Roy Clark come to mind), I'd just be surprised if they could get through the chord changes of 'Giant Steps' by John Coltrane, or Bill Evans' 'Very Early,' or Chick Corea's 'Tones For Joan's Bones,' or any number of tunes written by jazz masters that go through a myriad of key changes and use complex (and beautifully elegant!) harmonic structures. Although I do think Glen Campbell and Roy Clark could play those tunes if they chose to practice them! I think guys at that level could apply themselves to just about any style of music and be great. But for the majority of country players I'm pretty sure it's beyond their ability to handle tunes of that complexity. rhythm: simple, but not undeveloped.

The groove of country (and pretty much any popular music), while simple, can be deceptively simple. I have to give a nod to the subtleties of the rhythmic feel of accomplished country players' lyrics: semi-developed, I am not a lyricist, but it seems to me that the messages of almost all country tunes deal with pretty 'common man' fare. They're not exactly delving deep into the human soul. I love you, you love me, you done me wrong, etc. But then again, it's not my area of expertise so I could be way off base here.

Emotional message: like the lyrics, it seems to be about pretty mundane stuff. The music gets its fans pretty riled up and enthusiastic, but once again, my take would be that those people aren't really paying attention to the music *per se*, it's more about the 'way it makes them feel.'

So here I am, a jazz pianist, a specialist in the music field, like any other specialist, looking for something a cut above the ordinary. I've put a lot of thought and energy into music, the same way a scientist, or an author, or an oral surgeon have put a lot of thought and energy into their fields.

If a top-notch building contractor looks at a kitchen wall, he will see subtle flaws and construction details that would escape my notice. To him, one wall is far superior to another wall, even though they both perform the same function as a wall equally well. To me a wall is a wall. Two guys who are car specialists will discuss at great length a minor detail in a car. A motor part, a tiny alteration in a body design, something so insignificant to a non-car specialist that it seems almost ludicrous that these two guys would take the time to talk about it for a minute, let alone carry on a conversation for hours, and if they're friends, drag it out at times over periods of years. Golf, sports, cooking, fashion, home decor, tropical fish, the list of topics that one person thinks is trivial and another thinks is all-important is endless.

What does country music have for a specialist such as myself? It doesn't hit me emotionally, there's minimal melody for me to grab onto, the harmony is of nursery rhyme caliber, and I don't care a bit about lyrics. I'm not a poet. There's just not enough there for me."

(Silence for a moment.)

I: "Well. That's a mouthful. That's an unusual way to look at it. What do you mean by saying the harmony is of 'nursery rhyme caliber?' It seems to me that you could make some country-western people awfully mad with a statement like that."

Me, with a sigh: "I know, I know . . . it's hard to come up with descriptive phrases that don't sound insulting, when I'm really not thinking of it in terms of 'bad' or 'good.' I'm really trying to be as objective as I possibly can be.

Look, at the risk of getting too technical here, let me quickly illustrate what I mean. Let's take a phenomenally successful country song, 'Achy Breaky Heart.' This song made millions of dollars and spawned an international dance craze. You still hear it on the radio today, years after it was released.

The harmonic structure of 'Achy Breaky Heart' is (and here's the slightly technical part) the 'one' chord followed by the 'five' chord then back to the 'one' chord. If you don't understand the concept of the 'one' and 'five' chord business, don't worry about it.

Suffice it to say, the harmonic structure of the nursery rhyme 'This Old Man' is exactly the same. A little different harmonic rhythm (when the chords occur in the song), but the chord progression is basically identical. 'Mary Had a Little Lamb,' 'Three Blind Mice,' 'Itsy Bitsy Spider,' they all share a similar harmonic structure with the vast majority of country-western songs. 'Baa, Baa, Black Sheep' actually has more complex harmonies than 'Achy Breaky Heart!'

The guys in Nashville have a system of holding up one, two, four, or five fingers to another player on stage to indicate where the harmony is headed (one finger for the 'one' chord, five fingers for the 'five' chord, etc.). They couldn't do that if the basic structures of country tunes weren't so simple. And before you say it – no, I don't think simple equals 'bad!' Sometimes simple is exactly what's called for. But for me, not all the time! At some point, my ears need more than that."

I: "Hmm . . . Well then, in the interest of pursuing this a bit further, how would you break down some other styles of music besides country?"

Me: "Well . . . OK . . . let's see . . . rap and hip-hop, melody:

what melody? I guess you could count the bass line as a kind of melody, albeit an extremely repetitive one.

Harmony: undeveloped, once in a while somebody will throw in a dissonant note or two which I appreciate, but the overall harmony is almost nonexistent. Rhythm: sometimes very complex and very cool. The drum machine sound gets to me after a while, but on the whole I like and respect the grooves they get going.

Production value: highly developed! Lyrics and message: ugh (although I am aware that rap tunes with positive messages have been written. Even Christian rap! But I don't think these define the genre.)

How about rock?

Melody: I'd say semi-developed, even when there is a recognizable melody, usually it will be of a fairly mundane variety. For instance, the Beatles had strong melodies, but once again, compared to the instrumental jazz melodies, or the great melodies of classical masters, they sound pretty much like teeny-bopper, kid's music to my ears.

Harmony: undeveloped to semi-developed depending on the band, two-note guitar 'power chords' don't really count as harmony! Once again, bands like the Beatles used slightly more sophisticated harmony, but nothing to tickle my ears.

Rhythm: strong and powerful. Lyrics and message: it's a pretty big umbrella, rock, but apart from a comparatively few songs that seem to have a deeper meaning (compared to the hundreds of thousands of rock tunes that have been written, that is), most rock songs seem to stick to the "hook" formula. 60's rock had the anti-war message, etc., but again, it's really not my field, so I'm probably talking out of school here.

How about I break down my music of choice, jazz? And once again, it's a pretty big umbrella. I'm not talking about 'trad jazz' (like Dixieland,) or smooth jazz, or even avant-garde jazz (although I love it!), but the jazz of Bill Evans, Chick Corea, John Coltrane (who I've already mentioned), or Oscar Peterson, Charlie Parker, Miles Davis, McCoy Tyner, Keith Jarrett, Horace Silver - the list goes on and on.

I'd break it down this way, melody: fully developed, very sophisticated melodies, both written and improvised.

Harmony: fully developed, very sophisticated harmonies, able to be re-harmonized in literally thousands of different ways and still be true to the genre.

Rhythm: fully developed, as complex or as simple as music can be. Some jazz is as advanced rhythmically as any classical music written to date. Lyrics and message: instrumental jazz is not a lyricist's music. There are guys who would say that if a vocalist is present, it's not jazz. I'm not sure I totally subscribe to this attitude (having worked with some great vocalists for whom I have the deepest respect) but as a total fan of instrumental music I certainly understand where they're coming from. The essence of jazz, as I perceive it, is creativity, freedom, and expression, with a profound knowledge of music and years of dedicated practice from which to draw."

I: "Hmm, I never thought of music in this way. Do you think every piece of music needs to be broken down and analyzed like this?"

Me: "No, no, of course not. I don't think ANY piece of music needs to be broken down and analyzed like this! I will say again, this is just my own personal take on things, not an instructional program. When I hear music, my mind automatically analyzes what's going on. It always has.

I realized a long time ago that to the vast majority of people, music is kind of a mass of sound, a wall of organized noise that provokes an emotional response, if you will. There's a pulse that gets their toe tapping, and of course, the lyrics to give it some kind of meaning to which they can relate.

For example, a long time ago I was asked if I liked this pop song that was playing on the car radio. Of course it had almost nothing of what I look for in music, but I tried to find something positive to say. There was a little synth line that some studio keyboard guy had added, probably at the behest of some studio producer, so I said that I liked that synth line, it added a little color and specialness to the song.

The person who asked me if I liked the song stared at the radio for a second and said wow, I never noticed that before. This got me curious. I asked, do you hear the bass line? I sang a little of it as it played. And do you hear how the drummer is playing eighth notes on his hi-hat, and the bass drum figure, with the snare putting the backbeat on two and four? I played the drum beat on the dashboard of the car. Hear how the guitarist is comping behind the vocals, kind of a choppy, percussive lick? More of me now imitating the guitar.

I looked at this person and realized that they had never looked at music in that way before, hearing its component parts. To them it was a mass of sound emanating from a set of speakers that made them feel good, or feel sad, or feel like dancing, or laughing, or whatever.

My mind does not work like that. I've spent far too much time practicing, analyzing, reading, studying, and just thinking about music not hear all of the component parts, as well as how they come together. Or don't come together!

In fact, I have a theory that the great producers are actually able to switch their ears, so to speak, and hear music as the consumer hears it. Then, if something doesn't jibe with their 'consumer ears,' they can turn on their 'producer ears' and identify and correct the musical component that offends them. I don't know if this is true or not, but it makes sense to me."

I: "So this wall of sound, this non-analytical way of looking at music, you think it's a lesser way of listening?"

Me: "Not at all. Music is emotional. There's no getting around that fact. It's also intellectual. This is also a fact. It's like anything else, the more you put into it, the more you get out of it. Everyone goes through a musical maturation process.

Just think of the songs that touched you as a child, 'Twinkle, Twinkle, Little Star' or 'The Wheels On The Bus.' Then you left that behind as you discovered pop music, usually in late elementary school or junior high.

For my generation that was the Monkees, the Beatles, the

Jackson Five. Later on (usually) there's another phase as you discover (or choose) a direction not only in music, but in life. Maybe you head in the heavy metal direction, grow your hair long, wear the same t-shirt for weeks, rebel against your parents, or you discover rap and do all things associated with that crowd, or if you're a total high-school band geek like me you grow up loving jazz and classical music.

Unfortunately, it seems that most people's musical growth stops at some point in their life. Their music becomes the status quo and all the new junk that the kids are listening to is garbage. This is true of all generations. The youth of the 1890's with their 'Bicycle Built For Two' I'm sure thought that the 'Charleston' of the Roaring Twenties was tasteless, immoral crap.

The kids of the twenties I'm sure thought their music far superior to the big band era of the forties. We all know what happened when rock and roll hit the scene in the sixties. I would guess that the middle-aged ancient Greeks of the fourth century B.C. thought the new modes the kids were playing on their lyres were intolerable jungle music. And now I hear people in my age group saying the exact same thing about the music of the twenty-first century that our parents said about music in the seventies.

I think that the important thing is to listen, not to shut out new forms of music just because they aren't the old forms, to make a personal decision about it based on open-minded, non-biased listening. Then if you don't like it, so be it.

I have my way of listening, and I can tell you very specifically why I like or don't like a piece of music. But I can assure you that my opinion would be based on thought and thoughtfulness, not knee-jerk reaction. Obviously not all music is for everyone. If you hear music as a mass of sound coming from your car speakers, then that's the way you hear it. OK. The important thing is to listen, not just hear."

I: "That's an interesting way to put it, listen, not just hear."

Me: "That's a paraphrase of a saying I came up with to talk to less experienced musicians. It goes like this: '*Listening* is not the same thing as *hearing*, and *playing together* is not the same thing as playing *at the same time.*'"

I: "Hmm, could you expand on that?"

Me: "Sure. I've played with so many musicians over the years, and the experiences range from the sublime to the ridiculous. I'm amazed at times at the lack of listening that goes on onstage.

Let me put it this way: let's say you have a quartet – piano, bass, drums, and sax. At any given point during a tune, one of those instruments is going to be the 'front man.' During the sax solo, he (or she) is the front man, during the piano solo it's the pianist's turn to be the front man. Every little thing that the other three musicians play while the soloist is playing should be in absolute, total support of the soloist. Every little thing.

You need to subvert your ego unselfishly and completely for the benefit of the 'front man of the moment.' Does this mean you sacrifice your playing to be a sideman for the soloist? Of course not. The better player you are, the better sideman you can, and are likely, to be. The thing is your mental attitude about playing with a group. Every little thing you play, no matter how small or insignificant, should be in support of the front man. And, when you are the front man, every little thing everyone else plays should be in support of you. This is *playing together.*

So many times, you get guys playing away, sawing away at the chord changes, whacking away at the drums, and all of their attention is on their own instrument and maybe the three feet or so surrounding their bodies. Or their minds are somewhere else completely, on what they have to do the next day, their car breaking down, the girl (or guy) sitting at the bar. How is it possible for every note, every chord, every small sound you make to be in support of the soloist when you're not even listening to the soloist?

I would say to an amateur musician after a tune, 'so what happened after we played the head and went into solos?' The answer may come back, 'well, there was a sax solo.' 'Can you sing me one lick, one melodic fragment of that solo?,' I'd ask. The answer invariably would come back negative. They weren't listening. They were hearing, they heard there was a sax solo, but they weren't listening. They were real busy hacking away, playing at the same time as everyone else, but they weren't playing together with everyone else.

All you need is to have a few experiences of playing with guys that can really play, guys that have spent the time, have done the work, but also listen really hard onstage to be astonished at what some people think playing jazz is. It's not a marching band, you can't just play your part and the music comes together by virtue of a talented composer (even in large jazz ensembles, where it is more of a composer's milieu, there is intense communication going on as well as a lot of room for individual creativity, so the listening principle still applies. Just check out the old Thad Jones/ Mel Lewis Big Band recordings from the Village Vanguard! It's like a big band that played like a quartet.)

In jazz, you *are* the composer, every moment that you're playing, four people in a quartet composing together on the spot. How can you compose together if you're not listening to each other?"

I: "Wow. You're making me want to play jazz."

Me, grin: "Start practicing."

I: 'Well, it may be time to take a question or two from the audience. Anybody got one?"

("I" looks out at the audience where several hands have been raised. He picks one out of the crowd.)

I: "You there, come down to the mike and let's hear your question."

(A semi-scraggly, twenty-something year old, college-student type sidles down his row and approaches a pre-set microphone in the main aisle of the hall.)

Q: "Hi."

("I" and "Me" nod hello.)

Q: "Well, my question concerns whether or not your evaluation system takes into account the fact that these other forms of music that aren't jazz touch millions of people's lives. Literally millions more people are touched by popular forms of music than are by instrumental jazz. How can you justify the superiority, or 'full development' as you put it, of jazz as music when so many people don't get it, but do get the other forms of music?"

Me: "Ah, the old 'most people' argument. One of my favorites! My poor wife hears about it all the time . . . I hear people constantly using the phrase 'Well, most people would think . . . blah, blah, blah,' whatever the issue is that they are trying to validate by using the fact that a majority of people accept or agree with whatever opinion the phrase user is espousing.

So if the opinion of millions of people is a yardstick by which we would judge the quality of something, then I guess a restaurant like McDonald's must have really great food. After all, millions more people prefer to eat a Big Mac than would eat a salad. Or (dare I say it!) a tofu dish. Millions of people's lives are touched by the so-called reality shows on TV, like "Survivor" and "The Apprentice." Do you think reality shows are quality programming? 'Most people' voted for George W. Bush. You look like you'd be a fan of George Bush."

(Camera cuts to the student standing in front of the mike.)

Me: "The fact is, people use the 'most people' argument to argue for their position, then when 'most people' don't agree with their position, 'most people' are idiots. Next time you watch a show on TV and ask 'How can people watch this crap?,' remember that there are millions of people being touched by that show, or it wouldn't be on TV.

So how do you justify your low opinion of a popular TV show when millions of people are touched by it? I'll even go further: I think it might possibly be easier for me to formulate an argument that if 'most people' like something, it's more likely to be garbage then quality. I think I could find more examples of bottom level music, art, entertainment, you name it, that 'most people' support than high quality music, art, and entertainment."

Q: "Well, I don't really waste my time watching TV."

Me: "Really? 'Most people' do. How do you justify your attitude that watching TV is a waste of time when, as you put it, 'literally millions' of people are touched by it? Just because you think that it's a waste of time? I think there's a pretty close parallel between my attitude towards pop music and your attitude towards TV and (I would presume) junk food. With the exception that I think I probably have more respect and a more open mind about pop music than you do about TV!"

I: "OK, I think we need to give someone else a chance to speak. How about you?" (points to another audience member)

(A young, blond, attractive woman comes up to the mike.)

Q: "Hello."

("I" and "Me" nod.)

Q: "Well, I am a singer/songwriter and I find your analysis of music troubling. I love the type of music that I write and play. I love the music of other people that write and play in the same style that I do. This music has been a huge part of my life ever since I was in junior high school. How can you tear apart something that is so deep inside someone's soul?"

Me: "Hmm . . . you've asked a question that has several parts. Let's start with me reiterating that the whole analysis exercise that I took you through is only, and I mean really only, in my personal way of looking at music. And once again, it's a way that I've arrived at through thought and thoughtfulness, I'm not just contemptibly pooh-poohing other forms of music offhand. I really try to see the pros and cons of all music, what I consider to be the strong points and the weak points.

I think it's fantastic that you've found a musical genre that you can feel so deeply about. Just think of all of the people that don't have that gift. They miss out on a world of experience. It's just that the singer/songwriter genre doesn't touch me at all. I mean, occasionally I'll hear someone playing live that has a sparkle about them, but inevitably ten minutes later I'm ready to move on. 1 can only listen to the same four chords so many times!

Not to mention the fact that I am most definitely not a lyricist, nor am I particularly interested in lyrics, which I believe would kind of eliminate the whole point of the genre, if I'm not mistaken. I would ask you, can you accept the fact that instrumental jazz touches me as deeply as your music touches you?"

Q: "Of course."

Me: "Do you like instrumental jazz?"

Q (reddening a little): "Not really very much."

Me: "How can you say that about a music that is so deep inside my soul?"

Q, smiling: "OK, I get your point. But for me, there's no lyrics. It's hard for me to listen without words to express the music."

Me: "Yep, I am well aware of the phenomenon of lyrics and singers. Let me say this, I've given the matter of singers versus instrumentalists a lot of thought. Believe me, in my world it's an issue!

I came up with something that makes sense to me, I don't know if it would make sense to you or not but here it is anyway. I think that lyricists, and vocalists, are always searching for the 'perfect word.' The perfect word or phrase that perfectly captures what they're trying to put across in a song.

Conversely, if you read history, specifically music history, biographies and autobiographies of composers and whatnot, I think you'll find that the great composers, the Beethovens, the Mozarts, the Stravinskys, are all searching to express in their instrumental music that which cannot be put into words.

The minute you put a word to it, you've destroyed it. You've now reduced it to human terms, put it in a box, confined it in a cage. There's a saying (Chinese, I believe) that says 'the Tao that can be spoken is not the Tao.' I think they're saying the same thing that I am.

So you have this one group of people trying with all their might, with all their creativity, to find the perfect word, and this other group for whom words are anathema. No wonder there's a problem!

Another aspect of this rift is that in a vocal genre, the instrumental music is subordinate to the lyrics and voice. It is in a support role. Maybe a very important, irreplaceable support role, but a support role nonetheless. If any part of the instrumental accompaniment detracts or interferes with the vocals, it's gone. Like now.

They don't cut vocal parts to accommodate instrumental

parts (or if they do, it's very, very rarely). So you can see that your need for lyrics is exactly the opposite of an instrumentalist's desire to hear the cats play. In fact, I'll often be listening to the radio and think, man, get that vocalist out of the way so can hear these guys blow!

But I certainly understand and respect your values in music. You seem like you given it thought and care, and you have an air of sincerity about you. What more can you ask for?"

I: "Time for one more - how about you?"

(A well-dressed, thirty-sh man approaches the microphone.)

Q: "I'm actually in the music business, I own a small record label and have been in music in one way or another my whole life. I think that a lot of people who put down popular forms of music are in denial. Call it jealousy, sour grapes, whatever.

The fact is, the forms of music you've been analyzing (rap, rock, country, etc.) all make hundreds, if not thousands, of times the money that so-called 'art music' does. Bottom line is, everybody's looking for gigs, CD sales, Mp3 downloads, an appearance on late-night TV, a big house and car, and bucks in the bank. Jazz accounts for, what, 5% of the market? That figure actually may be high."

Me: "Ah, a 'money-worshipper.' Hey, you're right, everybody wants the house, the car, and all the stuff you said. Who wouldn't? But let's make sure we're talking about the same thing here.

If I were asked on this show to discuss music as a business, or profitability in the music business, you and I would probably have a great chat and go out to dinner afterward. But that's not why I'm here. I'm here to discuss music for music's sake, damn the economics.

The fact is, even 5% of the music industry is plenty of money for a musical genre to survive on. That's not the point. If you want to talk about money, let's talk about money.

What role does money have in your life? I'll tell you this: if I were to (God forbid) contract an incurable disease, or get an inoperable brain tumor, or lose a hand, I could own every dollar, every euro, every yen, every dinar in the world and it wouldn't do me a bit of good, except to make me more comfortable as I die. What's the importance of money in that case? If my wife were to leave me (of course, she'd probably leave me because I didn't have enough money, but that's another story!) I can't buy her love back.

I was a businessman who owned and operated a jazz club for four years. I'm pretty well acquainted with dealing with money on a daily basis. In its sphere, in business, money is God. The all-important, life's-blood of business. Outside of its sphere, it is nothing. Meaningless. You need to be able to separate the business of music (i.e.: money) from the art of music. And music, believe me, is an art. Of the highest order.

If you worship money, and think that monetary success defines quality, then where do you draw the line? Is a successful crack cocaine dealer to be admired? I think there are actually some businessmen who think so.

To use an analogy from earlier, McDonald's makes millions of dollars more than an exclusive restaurant in Manhattan. Am I to infer from that that their product, their food, is superior to the Manhattan restaurant?

Look, I admire a successful business model, admire smart business practices, but if you think for one second that money equals quality, then you're dead wrong. You just have to look around you to see that. Do you know how much money the pornography industry generates every year? Where do you draw the line?"

Q: "Oh come on, don't try to compare the music business to crack cocaine dealing and pornography. That's just ridiculous. Get real."

Me: "Actually, sir, I'm just about as offended by songs that glorify killing cops, and songs that encourage battering women, and music videos that promote racial hatred as I am about a crack dealer. If you think words don't have power to influence people, especially young people, then you're not as intelligent as I think you are. Maybe you don't like the police, maybe you beat your wife or girlfriend, I don't know. All I know is that when I hear

29

those songs, I have a visceral reaction, and I am filled with disgust."

Q: "Well, those aren't the songs I was talking about . . . "

Me, getting a little snippy: "Well, those tunes made millions of dollars, didn't they? Maybe you need to go rethink your position on money and music. Maybe using money as yardstick isn't really the smartest way to view things."

I, hastily interjecting: "OK . . . I think that'll just about do it for tonight, folks. We're out of time, I'd like to thank you all for coming to the show, and get home safely. A big hand for Kelly Park, ladies and gentlemen!"

(The sound of one hand clapping.)

You should know that I always win in my imaginary conversations, like I always win in an imaginary fistfight. I'm sure the reality would be much different.

# Chapter 2

## Apples And Oranges

"Intellectual growth should commence at birth and cease only at death"
— Albert Einstein

Let's suppose, for illustrative purposes, there are two people, one who loves apples and one who loves oranges, who get in a conversation. The apple lover passionately declaims the virtue of the apple, why it is the noblest of fruits, its incomparable virtues, the color, the taste, how could anyone not love an apple?

The orange lover counters with a flowery description of the orange, its heavenly nectar, its bright, cheerful hue, the sweet flavor like one would suppose a ray of sunshine would taste, how could anyone not love an orange?

Now, there are (at least) two ways this discussion could go.

In the first, the two people fall into a bitter argument, each trying to change the other's mind, each stubbornly sticking to his or her viewpoint to the extent that even if one person makes a point with which the other agrees, they won't agree for argument's sake.

Most likely, we've all been in discussions like this. At this point, the heavy artillery comes out, missiles are launched, and the war begins. It is a war that is pointless and unwinnable, but a war that is going to be fought anyway. The two people part as enemies, convinced of the utter stupidity and blockheadedness of the other person.

In the second, the apple lover listens to the orange lover's reasons for preferring the orange to his beloved apple and says, "Huh. Well, I can see how you could love oranges. Your reasons for loving them are sound, perfectly understandable reasons. I myself, however prefer apples. And here's why."

The apple lover then proceeds to enumerate the many aspects of the apple that he or she finds so alluring, after which the orange lover says, "Well. That's very interesting. I can see why you are an apple lover. You've pointed out many aspects of the apple which I had not considered before. Thank you. However, no matter how convincing your arguments for the apple are, I still prefer oranges."

The apple lover replies, "Hmm, well, I won't pretend not to be disappointed that I haven't changed your mind *vis-a-vis* the apple, but I can only put my reasons for thinking the apple is the best of fruits out on the table. I can't make anybody buy into them. Well, that was a very interesting discussion, I learned things about the orange I hadn't known before. Thank you. Would you like to go to a movie? You bring an orange and I'll bring an apple."

The two then proceed to go out to a lovely evening at the movie theater (but they probably got into an argument over what movie to go see!).

The second form of debate is by far my preferred method of conversation. I can argue my point of view vehemently, but if the other person doesn't agree, so be it. If the other person can raise a point that I hadn't previously considered, I'm more than happy to change or amend my viewpoint. If we can't agree on anything, we can agree to disagree, with no personal rancor involved.

I'm sure there will be people who will read the previous section, "Conversations #1," and will utterly reject the line of thinking that I put forth. They'll think that my way of looking at music is the most ridiculous thing they've ever heard.

That's cool. I don't have any pathological need to have people agree with me. I'd love to have a discussion (but only like in the second example above!) with anyone about it. Any time. I love intellectual discussion!

## Things That Bug Me #1

I hear people repeat the saying,

"Money is the root of all evil."

That is NOT the saying!

The saying is,

"The LOVE of money is the root of all evil!"

This is a completely different thing! Money is OK! Loving it too much is where all of the problems start!

# 0.5%

"Most people use music as a couch; they want to be pillowed on it, relaxed and consoled for the stress of daily living. But serious music was never meant to be soporific" – Aaron Copland

I can walk into a music club, just about any kind of music club, and if the players are good, get excited about the music. If I walk into a Dixieland room in New Orleans, my toes start tapping, the music fills me with joy, and I dig it. If I walk into a blues club in Chicago, and the cats are really playing, not just miscellaneous blues licks, but playing from the heart, I can be fascinated by the aura they create. A Cajun club, a rockabilly bar, a reggae club on the beach, a little liana on Maui featuring Hawaiian music, a salsa club, even (dare I say it!) a Euro nightclub with house music blasting from the speakers. It all has its own magic, its own slice of aural specialness.

But the problem for me is, fifteen minutes later I'm ready to move on.

The first Dixieland tune I hear as I walk into the club in New Orleans I'm saying to myself, "Wow, this music is fun! These guys can really play!" The second tune in I'm still tapping my toes and enjoying it. By the third tune my ears are getting restless. By the fourth tune I'm saying, "OK, now what?" I've heard pretty much the same type of rhythmic pulse, maybe slower here, maybe faster there, the chord changes are all kind of similar, once you've heard a couple of tunes you've kind of got the whole bag of tricks.

Now I'm ready for the next level. But there is no next level. After the first fifteen minutes, I realize that that's about it. Oh, there may be a novelty tune coming up that features the band singing or shouting, or beating on the tables, but for me that falls into the comedy entertainment world, the music is still pretty much the same. Now I'm bored.

This phenomenon happens to me at all of the venues mentioned above. I walk into a salsa club, woo-hoo! Arriba! Big fun for fifteen or twenty minutes, then my ears tap me on the shoulder and say, "Uh, boss? Can we hear something different now?" But I know that all night it's going to be more of the same. If there's a Zydeco band with a hot accordion player playing on an outside stage at a festival, I'm drawn to it. The cat can really play! Twenty minutes later I've heard basically all of the harmonies, have heard or can anticipate all of the rhythmic styles, and even the various licks that define the genre are sounding the same to my ears.

Ironically, the musical genre that I can sit and listen to all night long, and not get bored by, is probably the genre that bores the hell out of 99.5% of people! I can sit and listen to a piano trio, with guys that can really do it, all night long.

The harmonies, the textures, the rhythmic variety, the seriousness, the light-heartedness, the simple melodies, the complex melodies, the top-level professionalism of the playing, the hard listening going on, all combining to "make the whole greater than the sum of the parts" somehow satisfies the musical appetite in me. It is a far subtler music than any listed above, it requires mental participation and focus on the part of the listener to get the most out of the music.

Maybe that's one of the reasons it falls flat on many people's ears. I grew up in the first TV generation, my parents did not have TV as children. We learned to be entertained by the TV set, with no action or thought required on our parts. So much of what we experience in today's world is pounded into us, all we have to do is sit there, open mouthed and drooling, while information (much of which is of dubious quality) is hammered into our brains. TV is like a sledgehammer pounding on our heads. (Don't get me wrong, I'm still a TV addict! Some things never change ...)

But I'm actually one of the few parents I know that is not anti-video games. I think the participatory level of computer games is far greater than many of the pastimes in which we engaged as kids. My only beef is the amount of time my kids will spend being "interfaced" with the computer, I have to kick them off and get them outside, or doing some artwork, or reading a book, or (wow!)

practicing! (My son is a drummer and my daughter plays piano and flute.) (They actually are good practicers!)

But maybe that is why so many people can't listen to a jazz trio, a string quartet, or even a symphony orchestra without getting bored. The immediacy of pop music, the mindlessness of the simple rhythmic pulse, the fact that more complex music requires more from the listener as well as the performer, it all makes listening to pop music so much easier for the casual music listener. Oh yeah, and there's a singer and a song with a catchy hook.

I am well aware that my musical taste is shared by (possibly) (on a good day) 0.5% of the world's population.

I'm OK with it.

# Chapter 3

## The Great Divide

## A Few Quotes On Words, Language, Lyrics, And Instrumental Music

"If a composer could say what he had to say in words he would not bother trying to say it in music" - Gustav Mahler

"Music expresses that which cannot be said and on which it is impossible to be silent" - Victor Hugo

"After silence, that which comes nearest to expressing the inexpressible is music" - Aldous Huxley

"Music can name the unnameable and communicate the unknowable" - Leonard Bernstein

"Music is the only language in which you cannot say a mean or sarcastic thing" - John Erskine

"The whole problem can be stated quite simply by asking, 'Is there a meaning to music?' My answer would be, 'Yes.' And 'Can you state in so many words what the meaning is?' My answer would be, 'No'" - Aaron Copland

"Music happens to be an art form that transcends language" - Herbie Hancock

# Humor In Music

"Composition is slow improvisation and improvisation is very fast composition" – Arnold Schoenberg

Ah, there's nothing like a quote of "Pop Goes the Weasel" in the middle of a jazz solo to bring a smile to a person's face. Or a quote of a pop tune. Or "Chopsticks." Or "na, na, na, na, naaa, na." But good God, where does it end?!

There's a saying that contends that the pun is the lowest form of humor. I'd say the musical quote may give the pun a run for its money. Don't get me wrong, I'll play a silly quote now and then, every once in a while it's a welcome mood-lightener.

I played with a fellow in Michigan whose solos consisted of nothing but quotes, one after another after another. This was amusing and fun for the first two or three tunes. After that you wanted to shoot him.

Humor has a definite place in music, be it jazz, rock, or classical, but some people forget that: a) one man's comedy is another man's tragedy, and b) a joke ceases to be funny if it's told over and over and over again (unless maybe the telling is separated by an interval of time – like weeks or months ... or years).

Those players who have have no humor in their playing run the risk of taking themselves too seriously, a horrible state of affairs. But those players who constantly make musical jokes run an even greater risk – either losing or curtailing their ability to play a meaningful melody, or alienating other musicians to the point that no one but bottom level musicians will hire them. No professional wants to play with someone that constantly makes a mockery of music. Everyone draws the line at different places, but eventually their line will be crossed sooner or later by the habitual quoter or jokester.

When a player is trying to make a musical statement, something that actually means something to him, almost nothing destroys the mood like an untimely, inappropriate musical joke from another band member. I have seen fights erupt on stage because of this.

# Things That Bug Me #2

Oh . . . my . . . God . . . the guys that sell "Play the Piano In One Hour!" type seminars. Will the world never be rid of snake oil salesmen? I guess they've been around throughout the history of mankind. There was probably a Cro-Magnon that sold a Neanderthal a "special rock."

Hey, if you took one of those seminars and got something out of it, more power to you. But I'll bet with the money spent on one seminar you could have taken several private lessons with a local cat and gotten better information. I think there will always be a market for "Get Rich While Sitting around Doing Nothing!" seminars and "Learn to Be a Rocket Scientist in Your Spare Time!" CDs (with accompanying full-color booklet!), and I'm sure we will hear (yet again) about someone sending $7,476 to Nigeria to get a percentage of *$6,000,000.00!* that someone in Nigeria has in an offshore bank account. Sheesh!

I guess the people that buy this stuff sit around getting rich while playing all the piano they learned in one hour as the money from Nigeria gets wired to their bank. Then they take a break and learn how to be a rocket scientist.

# The Art of Practice

If there's one thing musicians know how to do, it's how to practice. No matter how crazy and scattered the other aspects of their lives may be (and believe me, that can be extremely crazy and scattered!), every musician that has taken his or her instrument to a high level of proficiency has, at some point in their lives, sat down with their instrument and practiced.

Every day, for hours a day. Many musicians are a strange combination of discipline and disorder. They'll have the discipline to sit and practice for eight hours a day (like I did for years as a kid) (on drums) (my Dad put me in a room far away from the rest of the family), but ask them if their checkbook is balanced and you might be disappointed. Not to mention their taxes!

At about the age of twenty-eight or so I started hearing from my contemporaries the phrase (in one way or another), "You're lucky, you always knew what you wanted to do." They were going through the normal angst of a young adult as they slowly (or suddenly) came to the realization that they wanted to find something that had personal meaning to do for a living.

The only problem was that they discovered that they hadn't taken the time to find something that really had any personal meaning for them. They'd been busy with all the stuff that goes along with being nineteen, or twenty-one, or twenty-five, and hadn't given a lot of thought to the future. The future's still a long way off when you're nineteen!

Then all of a sudden thirty looms. Sure, there's luck involved in making your living doing what you love to do, be it music, art, or dentistry. But mostly it's dedicated work and study that gets you there. I've known so many extremely talented people in my life, the situations in which I've found myself would almost guarantee that I would meet creative, gifted people.

I put myself in the sixty-five to seventy percentile of "born with it" talent. While not untalented, I've really had to apply myself to get to the level of music that I have attained. And I'm still practicing! And hopefully getting better.

So when I hear "You're lucky . . . " I always say, "Yes, I am." But guess what? Nobody wakes up in the morning and says, "Well I'll be darned, I can play the piano! Huh . . . I couldn't do *that* yesterday!" It's hard work to become proficient at a musical instrument! Unpaid!

I discovered the following quote from President Calvin Coolidge when I was in college, and it helped me when I'd feel inadequate being surrounded by some of the super talents with whom I attended Berklee College of Music.

It goes like this:

*Nothing in the world can take the place of persistence.*

*Talent will not; nothing is more common than unsuccessful men with talent.*

*Genius will not; unrewarded genius is almost a proverb.*

*Education will not; the world is full of educated derelicts.*

*Persistence and determination are omnipotent. The slogan 'press on' has solved and always will solve the problems of the human race.*

*No person was ever honored for what he received. Honor has been the reward for what he gave.*

# Be Like Bo

"I know you've heard it a thousand times before. But it's true – hard work pays off. If you want to be good, you have to practice, practice, practice. If you don't love something, then don't do it" – Ray Bradbury

"Practice, work hard, and give it everything you have" – Dizzy Dean

"If I don't practice one day, I know it; two days, the critics know it; three days, the public knows it" – Jascha Heifetz

"Practice does not make perfect. Only perfect practice makes perfect" – Vince Lombardi

"You practice Monday through Friday in college, or Monday through Saturday in the pros – and then you just go out and knock somebody's head off" – Bo Jackson

# Conversations #2

"All my ex's live in Texas and that's why I hang my hat in Tennessee" – George Strait

"For the introduction of a new kind of music must be shunned as imperiling the whole state; since styles of music are never disturbed without affecting the most important political institutions" – Plato (that middle-aged Greek guy from the 4th century B.C. who didn't like the new-fangled modes the kids were playing on their lyres?)

The scene: a country western bar in Texas into which, for some reason, I find myself going for a drink. From the outside, it looked like a Hollywood version of a "typical" redneck bar, located on the outskirts of town, its driveway peeling off from the far right lane before the highway on which it was situated disappeared into the oblivion of the Texas badlands.

There were a few pickup trucks (all of American manufactured), a couple of Harleys, and various and sundry Chevys, Fords, and Chryslers parked in a gravel-covered lot. The garish red, blue, and yellow neon signs that hung in the front window of the bar splashed color onto the hoods and windshields of the cars and trucks parked outside.

As I pushed the door open and entered the dim, smoke-filled room, I felt the eyes of the patrons give me the "once over" from under the brims of their Stetsons and John Deere-logoed baseball caps.

I walked up to the bar and plonked down onto the only available bar stool. My neighbor to the right was a beefy, all-American cowboy, from the tips of his cowboy boots, past his well-worn blue jeans and denim work shirt, to the black crown of his feather-banded cowboy hat. My neighbor to the left was an old man whose head lay on the bar, mouth hanging slack in a gap-toothed snore. Noon seemed to mind that he was passed out on the bar.

"What'll it be?," asked the bartender as he walked to the spot opposite me on his side of the bar. He held a beer glass in one hand as he polished it with a greyish bar towel with the other.

"Guess I'll have a beer," I replied. "What kind you got?"

The bartender looked me up and down, noting, no doubt, my Hawaiian "aloha" shirt, black Dockers, and grey tennis shoes.

"Bud, Bud Lite, Miller, Miller Lite, Pabst, and Lone Star," he finally offered.

"Hmm," I mused. "No Heineken?"

There was a guffaw from down the bar a ways.

"We don't cotton to that foreign shit here," the bartender said curtly.

"Well, then, make it a Lone Star, please," I said with a friendly smile.

He didn't smile back.

After getting my beer and taking a gulp to wash down the Texas dust, I relaxed a little and leaned my elbows on the bar. The sounds of a country guitar plinking away came from a fifties-style jukebox that stood against the wall.

As I sat there taking in the local color (and smell), I suddenly felt my neighbor-on-my-right's eyes on me.

I turned to see him studying me, his glacial, pale-blue eyes gazing steadily at my face.

"You're (*yore*) that piano player fella, ain't you? The one that wrote that book," he asked peremptorily.

"Well, yes," I replied, somewhat flustered that anyone out here in Nowhere, Texas would recognize me.

"Well, I read your (*yore*) book and I gotta tell ya, I think your fulla shit." His icy eyes never wavered from their steady gaze.

"Hmm . . . well . . . you know . . . everyone's got a . . . right to their opinion." I was mumbling and I knew it.

A head popped out from behind my neighbor and declaimed in a loud, shrill voice, "Don't yew know who this is, boy? This here is Clete "Ironhead" (*"Arnhaid"*) Gamble, the hottest damn *git-tar* player in the great state o' Texas."

There were rumblings of agreement up and down the bar.

"Ah," I murmured, "I'm sorry, I don't . . . I haven't really heard of . . . " my voice trailed off.

There was an uncomfortable pause.

Clete broke the silence, "It don't matter to me none if you know who I am or not. What ticks me off is that you don't seem to get the point of country music at all, son. Then you go and write about it in a book, like you know something. I mean, you go on and on about how the harmony is "undeveloped," and country music is like nursery rhymes, and the lyrics are banal (*bay-nel*) and you don't seem to realize that that don't mean shit to us. That ain't the point, son. You don't get it at all."

"Ah," I said, getting the gist of the matter. "I see. You seem to think that I don't get the point of country music."

His brow furrowed. 'Well, hell yes, boy. What you think I just said?"

I raised my hands in a placating gesture. "I'm just trying to be clear on your position. No worries," I smiled a cheesy smile.

He didn't smile back.

"Look," I said, placing my hands on the bar rail. "I think I actually do get the point of country music. I mean, I think I've played enough different styles of music and hung around with enough different musicians to get an idea of the points of many different styles of music. Will my concept be as deep or refined as someone who is steeped in the tradition of the music, someone who lives and breathes it? No, of course not. But I'm pretty confident that I can converse on a tolerably meaningful level with anyone about pretty much any style of music. And I hopefully would learn something myself, too!"

From the what-in-tarnation-is-he-talkin'-'bout look on the guy-behind-Clete's face, I might as well have been speaking French to one of those armadillos trundling about outside. Clete seemed to get it, though.

"Tolerably meaningful, huh?," he had a skeptical, somewhat derisive look on his face as he took a sip of his Lone Star.

"Well, yeah," I said. "I'm not going to pretend that I know all about a style of music that I really don't, but I think that on some level all Western music - not country-western," I hastily added,

"Western as in the European tradition of music - it all has similarities. We all use the same notes, harmonies, even instruments. You're a guitar player, right? Well, so were Joe Pass, Wes Montgomery, and Les Paul. Not to mention other guys like Andres Segovia, Antonio Carlos Jobim, and John Scofield. Those guys were (or are, in John's case) great players of your instrument, but in completely different styles."

Clete said, a bit grudgingly, "Yeah, them fellas were purty good players, I reckon. I got me a nice Les Paul guitar back home. It still don't mean that you got any kinda clue about country music."

I started to feel that maybe Clete and I could have a conversation. A couple of guys had gathered around us to listen in on the debate.

"Well, Clete ("Mr. Gamble?" "Clete," was the response, "Mr. Gamble is my Daddy.") "You seem like a smart, square-dealing, talented guy. Can I make a deal with you? If we have your conversation first, about the point of country music, can we have my conversation after that, about why I wrote what I wrote in my book?"

He thought for a minute.

"Well (*wa-a-a-l*), I s'pose we might. You may just learn a thang or two."

"I would be very grateful if I did," I said. Clete shot a sharp glance at me to see if I was being sarcastic.

"Really," I said, putting up my hands. "I actually have an open mind. It just appears as if it's closed most of the time."

He snorted.

"So tell me, from your perspective, what is the point of country music?" I asked.

Clete thought for a minute before speaking.

"Well, it ain't somethin' that we all sit around and talk about all the time. We jes' know it. Country music is what it is, son. It's the music of our people, the American people, the people you see around you here, and out on those streets."

He waved a hand in the air. "It's the music of our fathers and our grandfathers. It's the sound of our tradition of comin' out west, cowboys and settlers makin' a new country out of nothin'. With their bare hands. It speaks to the people, son, our people. When you get it, it's not in your head. It's in your gut, it's in your heart, it's in your *soul*. It cain't be talked about in words, really, you either get it or you don't. It don't matter if it's got no fancy chords, or fancy melody, it's dead simple, honest music, like the simple, decent, honest folk that we play for. That's the point, that we play for the people, our people, the people that built this country. If you don't understand that, then I don't know what you can understand."

"That's right (*raht*)!" "You tell 'um!" The sounds of encouragement came from all around us.

"Hmm," I said, 'Well, that's kind of what I already thought country music was about. I mean, I guess that's why they call it 'folk music', it's music for folks. Look, when I wrote what I wrote in my book, it was from the perspective of a specialist, a musicologist, if you will. I was trying not to let my personal tastes, preferences, or emotional leanings influence what I was trying to do, which was to write an objective, non-personal, non-biased assessment of different styles of music. It wasn't a statement as to the quality or superiority of any style of music over any other and it certainly was not intended to be a criticism or a negative reflection on country music, or any other kind of music for that matter. Except maybe some rap music, with the cop-killing and violence toward women and stuff."

"Rap music." "Shit." The crowd let its feelings be known. Someone spat on the floor.

Clete looked at me and said, "Well, that's just it, ain't it? I don't think you can talk about music without talking about what it means, son. If you leave that out, you leave out the part that makes it music. So then what's the damn point?"

"Ah, but I think you can talk about music without having to deal with its meaningfulness, or lack thereof. If anything, that's the point of departure between you and I, Clete," I said, "But that's 'my conversation', the one we agreed to have after 'your conversation'. If I were to have any problem with what you just said about the point of country music, it would be the use of the word 'American'. That word means a whole lot of things, Clete, and it's not just white folks from Texas who are Americans."

The guy at the bar behind Clete piped up, "Yew know, I thought yew looked mixed. Yew part Mexican (*Meskin*) or somethin'?"

"My father is from Hawaii and my mother grew up in Idaho," I replied, "And last time I checked, Hawaii was part of America ." I gave him a brittle smile.

"Well, hell, boy, we ain't all racists down here in Texas," Clete said, "I got some black friends I play music with and we get along just fine."

"Yeah, you didn't strike me as a bigot, Clete," I said, "It's just when someone uses the word 'American' to make a blanket statement, I always have to check to see what's being portrayed as being 'American.' I, probably like you with your career, have travelled all over this country and it's real hard for me to make a statement about 'Americans' that can be equally and truthfully applied to folks from New York City, as well as to folks from Wisconsin, or from New Orleans, or Juno, Alaska, or Seattle, or Maine, or Montana, the Arizona desert, the beaches of Hawaii, or Puerto Rico, or Guam, or to cowboys from Texas. And maybe most of all, that most 'foreign', wacky place in America, my home, the San Francisco Bay Area! But guess what? They're all just as American as anybody in this bar."

The crowd did not like this.

'Well now, that's true, 'bout them all bein' Americans," said Clete, "but I'm talkin' 'bout the Americans that built this country. The pioneers, our grandaddies and great-grandaddies who endured hardships and persevered and made this the greatest country in the world."

"Oh, you mean Europeans," I said, "You know, on my mother's side, we've traced our ancestry back to the early seventeen-hundreds on this continent. She was mostly of Norwegian and English descent. One of my ancestors signed the Declaration of Independence.

On my father's side, we think that his grandparents came to Hawaii from Korea (but we haven't traced that side of the family back). He and his parents were born in Hawaii. Tell me, what's the difference between Norway and Korea from the perspective of people emigrating to a new land? Any way you look at it, we're all foreigners here, or to put it another way, we're all Americans here. We all came from somewhere else.

The Native Americans, the 'Indians', would be the closest ones to really have a claim to being 'Americans', but it's been pretty much proven that they came over from Asia when there was a land bridge from that continent to Alaska, so even they, in a sense, are immigrants! My ancestors were here when almost all of your ancestors," I pointed around the room. "were still picking potatoes in the old country. Does that make me more American than you?"

The crowd didn't like this either.

Clete looked down at his beer glass. "I think we may have gotten off the point of country music a smidge," he said. "I still don't think you really understand how country music makes people feel inside. It makes grown men cry, it takes someone who's just had something awful happen in their life and helps 'em realize they're not alone, it's got nothin' to do with the notes and chords, it's the *realness* of country music that makes it what it is."

"Well, I thought that I had made that clear in my book, that I can see why all forms of music appeal to different people, but maybe I could have made it clearer. I mean, you guys live down here in Texas, you hear Mexican music all the time. Don't you think that that music hits the Mexican people the same way country music hits your fans? Don't you think that some Mexican folk music makes grown Mexican men cry? Makes them realize they're not alone and helps them through bad times? I mean, it seems pretty obvious that all folk music hits the people, the 'folk' of the genre description, in the same way.

I think that in Hungary, Hungarian folk music brings out the essential 'Hungarian-ness' of those people. If you go to a Greek wedding you'll see, in a very boisterous way, how those people respond to the music of their culture, even though it doesn't do a thing for you. Jewish music, Chinese music, Javanese gamelan orchestra music, it all hits 'their people' on the same gut level that country music hits you. Don't you think?"

"Well, mebbe," said Clete dubiously, "I don't want to say that we're any better than those folks ..."

"Yes, we are!" a shout came from the crowd, with general laughter.

"No, you're not," I said mildly.

The crowd grew ominous.

"Look," I said, ignoring my growing peril. "This conversation was about whether or not I got the 'point' of country music. You were pretty darn sure that I didn't have a clue at the beginning of our talk, what do you think now? I'm sure I don't 'get it' nearly as well as you, or even these guys here in this room," I waved my hand at the room in general. "But have I convinced you that at least I can see and appreciate (if not truly understand) the meaning of country music to you?"

"Well, I gotta admit, you got a better idea than I gave you credit for before," said Clete, "Even if you'll never get it, seems like you at least got respect for it."

"Absolutely I have respect for it," I replied, "And thank you for seeing that, I really appreciate it. So now ... can I try to explain why I wrote what I wrote in my book? 'My conversation'?"

Clete cocked his head and said, "Well, bring it on then, pardner."

I turned to the bartender who had been standing behind the bar listening to the debate and said, "Couple more Lone Stars, please, I'm buying!"

As he set the beers down on the bar top I turned to Clete and said, "Well, pardner (I was trying to get the hang of this Texas lingo), the first thing that you need to know about where I'm coming from musically is that the music I listen to is not vocal music. Do you sing as well as play?"

"No, I ain't much of a singer," he replied, "We got a rhythm guitarist that sings, and then a gal singer out front."

"Great, it's a lot harder for me to talk to vocalists and lyricists about music than it is to instrumentalists like yourself. When vocalists and I get in discussions, we tend to get bogged down in the 'singer vs. musician' thing, or the conversation goes into the field of lyrics, which interest me mildly, but not really that much. The music itself obviously speaks to you, and I'll bet you can make that guitar talk plenty without words."

He smiled.

I continued, "So we are not that far apart, you and I, we're both players, not singers. Difference being, my direction has always been towards jazz and classical music while you've taken country guitar to a very high level. We both know what it's like to sit and practice for hours, to listen and choose what we value in a player, we both have spent a lot of time and energy thinking about music. Just different genres of music. This is one of the facets I was talking about when I said on some planes, all music is the same. If you don't spend the time, no matter what the style of music, you won't take it to the highest level you can. No matter what style of music a player is playing, if he's good, he's good. If he's a player, he (or she) is a player. Would you agree with that?"

Clete thought for a minute then replied, "Well now, lemme tell ya, I've spent more time with my guitar than with my wife. I'd have to say that I agree with what you just said, maybe with the idea that 'good' to one person ain't always 'good' to another. There was a fella one time came out here from Oklahoma and everyone thought he was such a great guitarist, but I thought he couldn't play for shit. He was real fast, lightning fingers, but there warn't nothin' there, just a bunch of real fast notes. I couldn't say too much though, cuz everyone'd think I was jealous or somethin'."

"That's just what I was talking about!" I said eagerly. "You've obviously spent time thinking about what you value in music. When you were a kid you probably would have worshipped that guy.'

"Oh yeah, when I was a kid, I'd a thought he was the greatest thing since sliced bread," Clete grinned.

"Exactly," I said. "So you, as a country guitarist, about as far away from my musical taste as you can get, have those qualities that I, personally, respect in a musician. This is great, now we're on a level of conversation at which I can operate," I hastily added. "Not that the things that I personally respect are the be-all, end-all of music. It's just my take on it, not some kind of universal truth."

"Hell, pardner, I think those things are things all us musicians respect. Nobody I know respects some raggedy-ass player trying to pass himself off as a professional."

I grinned. "And we all know those cats!"

Clete bobbed his head. "We shore do."

"OK, so my conversation is based strictly on a 'nuts-and-bolts' level of music. If possible, let's take all thoughts of meaning, point, and all that subjective stuff and put it aside for now. One of the first things you said to me was how I compared country music to nursery rhymes and said that the harmony was 'undeveloped'. I hope you remember also how I wrote that if I could find other less negative terms to use, I would. I certainly didn't mean 'undeveloped' in any negative sense, but I realize it's hard not to perceive it as such.

So, that said, let me ask you, do you guys use the 'Nashville' way of indicating chords? How they'll hold up one finger for the 'one', or 'home' chord, and four fingers for the four chord, five fingers for the five chord, two for the two chord (which almost always really is the V7/V, not the diatonic two chord, but that's neither here nor there)? You guys use that?"

Clete said, "All the time, pardner. If we're in 'E', I'll hold up five fingers and my bass player will head straight for a 'B'."

"Exactly!" I exclaimed. "That's what we, in jazz and classical theory, call 'Roman Numeral Analysis.' If you build chords within a key, they will always come out to have the same intervallic relationship, regardless of the 'note name' of the chords. In 'E', 'B' is five, in 'G', 'D' is five, etc. Now if I take a nursery rhyme like 'Twinkle, Twinkle, Little Star' and apply the Nashville chord system to it, it would look like this:

(hold up one finger) Twinkle, twinkle,
(hold up four fingers) little
(hold up one finger) star
(hold up four fingers) how I
(hold up one finger) wonder
(hold up five fingers) what you
(hold up one finger) are
(hold up one finger) up a≠
(hold up four fingers) bove the
(hold up one finger) world so
(hold up five fingers) high
(hold up one finger) like a (hold up four fingers) diamond
(hold up one finger) in the
(hold up five fingers) sky
(hold up one finger) twinkle, twinkle,
(hold up four fingers) little
(hold up one finger) star
(hold up four fingers) how I
(hold up one finger) wonder
(hold up five fingers) what you
(hold up one finger) are

Now how many country songs are going to have, if not the same harmonic structure, a very similar harmonic structure to that?"

Clete thought for a moment. "Well, hell ... all of 'em, or most of 'em anyways."

"And that's all I meant by the nursery rhyme comparison. Now, I know it's not only that it's just one-to-four-to-five, it's what you do with the one-to-four-to-five that counts. But looking at it from the 'nuts-and-bolts' perspective that I laid out at the beginning of this conversation, that's what it is. The basic harmony of country western music is pretty much the same as the harmony of kids' nursery rhymes. Not what you do with the harmony - just the harmony itself, the notes and chords."

"Well, so what?" demanded Clete. "What do I care about fancy harmony? The music is what hits home to me."

"Right. Exactly," I said. "That's exactly why you shouldn't take what I wrote in the book personally. You've found what hits home for you. The book was about my own way of looking at music, not yours, not his (pointing at the bartender), not some Indian guy in New Delhi's, just mine. I personally can only listen to one-four-five chords for so long and my ears get bored. Add to this the fact that I'm not (as I pointed out earlier) a vocalist or lyricist, so what does country music have for me?

I don't know your work schedule, but I've done an average of 250 to 300 gigs a year for 35 years (and this is a conservative estimate, it's probably more, but I don't want to be accused of over-dramatization), that's 8,750 to 10,500-plus paid musical engagements in my life (so far!) – I get tired of one-four-five! I want to move forward, hear new stuff, new sounds, I don't want music to coddle me, to make me 'feel good.' That's not what I play or listen to music for. On many of my gigs I will play music to coddle people, and I actually like some of the commercial stuff I play, but that's the professional side of me coming out. I play for the situation in which I find myself to the best of my ability, for the people that hired me and the people that are listening to me. I play the gig."

Clete said, "10,000 gigs," he shook his head. "That's a lot of gigs. I play a lot, but not quite that much."

"Yeah, that's the life of a piano player," I replied, 'We can work six or seven nights a week, week in, week out. Then the holidays hit and it's crazy."

"Like when we go on tour and hit twenty-six different towns in twenty-six days. But then we take a month off," Clete said.

"Yeah, it's the same but different," I agreed, "I won't take a month off, but I hit the same town for twenty-six different days." I smiled.

"Now, correct me if I'm wrong, but didn't I read somewhere that Mozart wrote 'Twinkle, Twinkle, Little Star'?" asked Clete.

I grinned. "Yep. But it may be just a legend."

Clete said, "Well, then, I guess y'all'd have to classify Mr. Mozart's harmony as 'undeveloped' then, wouldn't ya?"

I answered, "Well, I don't know if I can go that far. He used a lot of harmonic devices in other pieces that were far more sophisticated than that. And, I believe, legend has it that he wrote 'Twinkle, Twinkle' when he was only five years old. Hardly a mature musician yet!

But actually, to answer your question, Mozart's harmony *isn't* nearly as developed as the harmony that came later in history. The Claude Debussys, Richard Strauss', and Igor Stravinskys of the world had Mozart on which to build. I tend to view music from a historical perspective. In other words, just because something sounds stale or outdated to us today doesn't mean it wasn't daring and fresh and groundbreaking in its time.

In your genre, I really like guys like Hank Williams, Sr. and Woodie Guthrie, there's a raw authenticity to their music, their music hadn't been in the air before, they were a new sound, a new musical perspective. Same with the old blues guitarists, and the early blues and boogie-woogie piano players, or even Elvis. In their time, what they were playing hadn't been heard before, they were the innovators, the inventors, the 'pushers of the envelope.' That I find to be deserving of the highest respect, to find something actually new to put in the air. I certainly haven't found it yet!"

"Yep, that's one of the hardest things, finding your own voice," Clete agreed.

"So Clete, have I changed your mind at all? Do you view my book in a different light than before? Am I still full of shit?"

"Yes!" The crowd voiced its opinion before Clete could answer.

"Hmm ... mebbe you'd best head for the door, pardner," Clete said, jerking his thumb in the direction of the front door, the route to which was unfortunately being blocked by several large bodies, topped by none-too-friendly faces all turned in my direction.

[At this point I have no way of writing an ending for this without getting my ass kicked, so I will use the time honored writing device of deus ex machina and have the police arrive just in time to escort me to my car for a fast getaway, or maybe I went all karate, spinning, kicking, punching, and flying through the air, leaving bodies lying on the floor gasping for breath as I fought my way to the front door and out to my fire engine-red Ferrari Testarossa. Hmm, I'll work on it.]

# Lyrics Have NOTHING To Do With Music!

Oh the blasphemy! In this world where music has become more and more identified with singers (coinciding with the advent of "reality" shows like American Idol and The Voice), I can feel the hackles rising on the neck of the reader who identifies with music as a vocal medium. I would beg their indulgence to merely consider two short scenarios that illustrate my point.

In the first, let's suppose we have a set of excellent lyrics; powerful, meaningful, and poignant. The lyricist takes his or her lyrics to a musician to set them to music, but the mediocre music fails miserably to support the lyrics. Believe me, this happens all the time!

So when the lyricist plays the song for people, the general reaction is a shrug of the shoulders and maybe a "Well, I like the words but . . ." In this case the music actually is a detriment to the words! Now the lyricist give his (or her) lyrics to a master actor who presents them to an audience as spoken word. His ability to convey the depth of the text to move people makes the audience weep and he gets a standing ovation. What on earth did those words have to do with music? The lyrics in this case actually benefitted greatly from the *absence* of music.

In another example, suppose there is a master sculptor. This person can work magic with a hammer and chisel and a piece of marble, but he can't paint to save his life. Now near him lives a master painter, a person who can blend line and color to create masterpieces of painting, but can't sculpt one bit.

One day the sculptor calls the painter to come paint one of his sculptures and the painter agrees. The painter does her usual excellent job and *voila*, they collaborate to create a wonderful piece. Now this piece isn't "sculpture" and it isn't "painting," but maybe a different genre like "painted sculpture." Point being, their collaboration doesn't make the painter a sculptor or the sculptor a painter. The two disciplines are still completely different, separate skill sets.

The same is true in music. Putting words to music doesn't make a lyricist a musician and it doesn't make a musician a lyricist, the two disciplines are completely separate. Just because they're combined to form a different genre (vocal music?) doesn't make them synonymous.

Lyrics are not music!

# Things That Bug Me #3 (Seriously!)

"You don't play music with your fingers, lips, or other bodily appendages, you play music with your heart, your mind, and your gut. You don't listen to music with your ears, you use the same organs to listen to music as you use to play it." – Kelly Park

I run across so many people who seem to think that "acting" serious is the same as "being" serious. One can take things lightly, laugh, act the clown and be dead serious about the things that one takes seriously.

So many people are taken in by a musician who has perfected the art of coming across as a heavy hitter, who really might be a very average, or below average, player. Those musicians with a cocky confidence that fools people into believing that they are making a meaningful musical statement, BS their way through tunes, finish off a non-sensical or completely pedestrian solo with a confident flair, often to great approval . . . except from the other musicians sharing the stage with them (or out in the audience).

Dizzy Gillespie could clown it up with the best of them, but when the rubber hit the road, he was all business. Lee Trevino would crack jokes all the way down the fairway, but when it came time to hit the ball, his total concentration was on doing his job.

IMHO (internet-speak) (my kids teach it to me), life is too short not to enjoy, but a big part of that enjoyment is the fulfillment of having something in your life that you take seriously. But just because you take it seriously doesn't mean you can't have a barrelful of fun doing it! Beware the musician that is trying to pull the wool over your eyes! (And ears!)

# Music Theory

"Hell, there are no rules here – we're trying to accomplish something"
– Thomas Alva Edison

"If you obey all the rules you miss all the fun" – Katherine Hepburn

Music theory is a favorite subject of mine. I find it fascinating, the different approaches one finds as one reads and studies. Early counterpoint, the study of harmonic devices used during different periods of history, Schönberg's twelve-tone system, atonal music, pitch-set theory, they all intrigue me.

I've dabbled in many theoretical genres, I've tried to understand what the heck they're talking about on websites like the 'Society For Music Theory' (I've even e-mailed some of those guys – and gotten an answer back!) Alas, my classical harmony isn't quite strong enough to jump in and swim with those cerebral cats. I did teach theory and harmony at the Berklee College of Music so my jazz chops are pretty good.

It's interesting to see how all Western music has built upon the music that came before it. We all stand on Bach's shoulders! I used to pound the piano in class and yell, "There's only twelve notes! Twelve notes! And then they're repeated! (pound!, up an octave) And repeated! (pound!) And repeated! (pound!)"

I had students that would transfer into my classes, and students that would transfer out of my classes. I've noticed that the study of music theory is one of the most intimidating subjects that people encounter when they first start exploring music. Do not be intimidated!

The nice thing is, is that the groundwork for Western harmony was developed during "The Age Of Rational Thinking" and "The Enlightenment" of the eighteenth century (Bach, 1685 - 1750.) Music theory makes sense! It is a logical, reasonable system that one has only to learn the language of to understand.

We use twelve notes in our system, no more, no less, and we're not likely to add or subtract another note in the foreseeable future. It is a "closed system." Once you learn the twelve notes, and their intervallic relationship(s) to each other, that's it. What you do with it, well, that's a different story!

Another diatribe from my teaching days: "Music is funny. One the one hand, it is totally rational. Twelve notes, arranged in half steps, tempered octaves for our ear. On the other hand, music is completely irrational.

If someone says they get their musical inspiration from the planet Pluto (I still think of it as a planet), who am I to say they don't? For all I know, there's a bunch of aliens sitting around on Pluto beaming melodic motifs at Earth. I just wish they'd beam some my way!" I think that's one of the greatest attributes of music, this dichotomy of the utterly rational and utterly irrational living side by side, indeed, inseparably attached to each other.

One of the main obstacles that I see in the student's path when they first assay to learn music theory is the fact that many of the people who teach the subject really don't have a grasp of it themselves.

I attended a local university for a year and a half after high school (then quit to play in a disco band - this was the seventies! But that's another story . . . ) and took some theory classes as required courses. It wasn't until after graduating from Berklee and then, really, teaching at Berklee, that I realized that the professors I had had at that time had, at best, a fuzzy concept of the subject. Oh, they knew what they were talking about, in a general way, but not so they could present it in a clear, concise manner for beginners to understand. The field is rife with this phenomenon.

It is possible to present music theory with a logical, building-block methodology that takes all of the "mystery" and confusion out of the subject. There's nothing mysterious about the twelve black-and-white keys on a piano! It's right there for one to see. What a talented person does with those black-and-white keys – ah . . . now *that's* true mystery.

# The Jazzmen (and Women!)

"A jazz musician is a juggler who uses harmonies instead of oranges"
– Benny Green

"Don't play what's there, play what's not there" – Miles Davis

"It's taken me all my life to learn what not to play" – Dizzy Gillespie

"You can play a shoestring if you're sincere" – John Coltrane

"In my music, I'm trying to play the truth of what I am. The reason it's difficult
is because I'm changing all the time" – Charles Mingus

"I can't stand to sing the same song the same way two nights in succession. If
you can, then it ain't music" – Billie Holiday

"If you don't make mistakes, you aren't really trying" – Coleman Hawkins

"There is no such thing as a wrong note" – Art Tatum

"Wrong is right" – Thelonious Monk

"It's the group sound that's important, even when you're playing a solo. You not
only have to know your own instrument, you must know the others and how to
back them up at all times. That's jazz" – Oscar Peterson

*Kelly Park*

# Chapter 4

## A Favorite Parable (and A Quiz!)

### A Favorite Parable

This parable, while simple and possibly naive, has stuck with me for many, many years. It seems to apply to so many situations especially out here in the "new age" San Francisco Bay Area, California.

It goes like this:

Three blind brothers came across an elephant in their travels. One brother felt the elephant's leg.

"An elephant is like a tree," he cried, "I know it because it's right here, under my hands, as real as the nose on *my* face!"

"Nonsense," replied his brother, "an elephant is like a wall (he had discovered the elephant's side, and was running his hands all over its large body), "I know it because I can feel it, I can put my hands on it, it's as real as the nose on my face!"

"You're both wrong!" yelled the third brother, who had found the elephant's trunk, "An elephant is like a snake! I'm holding it right now even as we speak."

Well, needless to say, the three fell into a big fight, whacking each other with canes and kicking each other in the shin. Each knew he alone was right, his position was not based on mere faith, but on an actual, tactile experience, a solid reality from which no one would ever be able to dissuade him.

"It's like a tree!"

"No, no, a wall!"

"You're both idiots, it's like a snake!"

Finally, exhausted, all three collapsed on the ground, battered and bloody. They lay on the ground feebly swiping at each other with their broken canes, and aiming half-hearted kicks at each other's shins.

The elephant, who had been completely oblivious to all of the goings-on around him, decided he was tired and lay down on his side, crushing the three brothers to death.

# A Quiz

And now the quiz!

From this parable can we say:

    a) We as humans cannot see the whole reality of something bigger than our senses can comprehend, no matter how real our experience of it seems to be?

    b) Using the elephant as a symbol of God (or a Higher Power if you prefer) and the brothers as symbols of humankind, can we refer to the leg, the side, and the trunk as different religions, extrapolating from there that all religions are a part of a greater truth?

    c) Can we infer from the story that if we can't allow other people to have their own truths, even if they are in contradiction to our own, that eventually we will beat the crap out of each other and in the end be crushed?

    d) That we as humans can fight and argue as much as we want, it doesn't really make a lot of difference because in the end we all wind up under the elephant?

    e) All of the above?

    f) None of the above?

All of the above?

"I have no pleasure in any man who despises music. It is no invention of ours: it is a gift of God. I place it next to theology. Satan hates music: He knows how it drives the evil spirit out of us" – Martin Luther

"The most important thing I look for in a musician is whether he knows how to listen" – Duke Ellington

"Master your instrument. Master the music. And then forget all that bullshit and just play" – Charlie Parker

# Chapter 5

## Final Thoughts on Lyrics, Vocalists, and Musicians

I addressed this topic earlier in the chapters entitled "The Great Divide" and "Lyrics Have NOTHING To Do With Music!", observations on the complicated relationship between vocalists, lyricists, and musicians. I'd like to expand on this a bit further on a more metaphysical level.

Most people believe in a power greater than humans, be it the Christian God, the Hebrew God, Allah, a Higher Power, the pantheon of Hindu deities, or maybe the Force from Star Wars. There are people who don't believe in any of this. This chapter is not for them.

In my long life of playing music and accompanying many, many singers, it seems to me that vocal music tends to be an expression of human emotion and human soul. The singers delve into themselves and find voice to express what's inside of them. Solo instrumentalists can be very similar to this. But I believe that the great compositions that have stood the test of time and survive to our day and indeed, will still be being played a hundred years from now, not only can have this human expression but also reflect a bit of that higher power, whatever one believes that is. Or more likely, a reflection of a reflection of a reflection of that universal force.

I think of this as "intra-human" and "extra-human."

The topics that 90% of lyrics deal with are, in my opinion, "intra-human." As everyone knows, the vast majority of songs are about love. New love, lost love, hopeful love, the list goes on. And I believe the vocalist delivering this message is emoting sympathetically with the lyrics and connecting with the audience on that very human level.

The feeling one gets as one enters say, a religious temple (depending on your beliefs), or maybe standing at the edge of the Grand Canyon, or gazing through a telescope at the billions of stars in the universe, can fill a person with a feeling that maybe there is something greater than humans in the universe (although to some people the Grand Canyon is just a big hole in the ground). This feeling I call "extra-human." Maybe it's more easily put as "intra-human" seems to be emanating from within a person outward, "extra-human" seems to be permeating a person from outward in.

Now does that mean there is no vocal music that does not have extra-human elements as well? Of course not. Or does that mean I believe all instrumental music taps into some mystical universal force? That would be ludicrous. But in general, I believe my observations are correct.

In an earlier chapter of this book, I quoted the Chinese saying that states "the Dao that can be spoken is not the Dao." This concept is what limits vocal music to being primarily intra-human. If you put words to something, it tends to take it out of the realm of extra-human and into the intra-human. You hear this all the time with lyrics applied to instrumental jazz tunes. Conversely, this very same concept is what frees the composer of instrumental music to stay in the realm of extra-human.

If the writers and fans of lyrics and poetry are bristling right now, I understand. Yet almost every poet or writer at some point has penned the idea that "mere words cannot express the way I feel" or "there are no words to say what I'm trying to say." Is this just BS? Just a flowery way to seem profound? I think not.

Words are confining! Powerful, but for the most part limited to our small (in comparison to the universe) human experience. As a musician, I find the ability of music to even grasp the slightest sliver of that extra-human, "greater than us" thing that's out there, extraordinary.

# In Closing

Am I a musical snob? Absolutely.

Is a race car mechanic an elitist when it comes to cars? Is a horse trainer unbelievably picky when it comes to judging horses? Have you ever watched a dog show? A fashion show? A cooking show? Do fine art critics get down to excruciatingly minute details when critically examining a piece of art?

Of course.

All specialists, no matter what the field, narrow their parameters, recognize what they judge to be excellence in their respective disciplines, and form their opinions accordingly.

A NASCAR pit boss might have pictures of matadors and crying clowns painted on black velvet hanging in his living room, for him art is just a way to cover up a hole in the wall. And a fine art critic may drive a twelve-year-old Yugo with a bad transmission, for him a car is just a way to get from point "A" to point "B", but within their specialties they give no quarter. There is no grey area between what they consider, through dedicated study and hard work, to be the best and the rest.

For some reason, music seems to be a subject upon which moderately to completely uneducated (musically) people will pronounce absolute judgments. People who would never dream of contradicting an expert in the field of, say, mathematics, will say with absolute authority that so-and-so is great music while this-and-that isn't music at all. I have no idea why this is.

Is it because music is so readily accessible, so omnipresent in our daily lives? Is it because they believe that music isn't as deep a discipline as mathematics? (I would bet a cookie that no mathematician would say that the music of Mozart isn't as deep and complex as mathematics!)

Is it because when music makes somebody feel an emotion, actually experience it just by hearing notes in the air, they get a sense of ownership, like they've come to a deep understanding of music because they were touched inside by it? (see the preceding parable!) It is a mystery to me.

I guess what it comes down to for me is, if one doesn't understand it, hasn't taken the time to study it, hasn't given it some real thought, don't pass judgment on it. All through the little journey of this book I've tried (and hopefully succeeded) to look at music objectively, without judgments of "good" or "bad." I (like everyone who cares about music) have my own personal tastes, my own very strong opinions on the subject, as I have a right to have, as everyone living has a right to have. I've done my best to illustrate why my take on music is what it is, that my opinions are evolved from decades of study, practice, playing, and immersion in the world of music.

If I have come off as judgmental, I thoroughly apologize. I actually see the charms of all music (well, maybe not the cop-killing stuff, I have way too many friends on the job), why people would be touched by rock and roll, new age, country, Dixieland, Latvian folk music, Argentinian tango, whatever. It just is not for me. Why? . . . well, I won't go into THAT again!

Thank you so much for taking the time to read my humble opuscule, if I could hope for anything, it would be that someone who previously had dismissed the musical genre known as jazz might listen in the future from a different angle, with fresh ears.

It is truly a marvelous art form, unfettered creativity combined with technical expertise, combined with sensitivity and taste, combined with furious energy, combined with melody, harmony, and rhythm at the highest level, combined with spontaneity, humor, thoughtfulness, and spirituality, all mixed together to form a cohesive, complete, and highly evolved art form. A living, breathing art form, as fresh nightly as the performers who are playing can make it.

Happy listening!

# Appendix
## A New Dictionary

**a capella** – Italian, translation: where the hell is the band?

**aphonesia** – noun, 1) the affliction of dialing a phone number and forgetting whom you were calling just as they answer. 2) getting to the end of a list of options on a recorded helpline number, only to forget which option one wanted; forcing one to listen to them again, and in some cases having to hangup and redial the number (related to *"senior moment"*)

**bebopulate** – verb, to change the style of any existing piece of music into bebop by taking the existing melody and adding jazz "riffs" a la Charlie Parker and Dizzy Gillespie (see "hipatitus")

**contemplative** – adj., upon deep reflection you decide that something really does suck

**hipatitis** – noun, a disease characterized by terminal coolness

**misunderhear** – verb, to not understand and not hear at the same time (past tense: misunderheard)

**nonversation** – noun, a conversation between two or more people with no intrinsic value (like the persiflage before, during, or after a musical gig)

**nostralgia** – noun, a reminder of one's past brought on by a familiar scent

**skeptimism** – noun, optimism that one has doubts about (rel. to "optimiskeptical" and "skeptioptimistic")

**telecrastination** – noun, the act of putting off making a phone call

**unanimosity** – noun, the result when everyone is in agreement, but nobody likes what they agreed upon